bloom.

Nicole Cloyd

To my high school English teachers.

sprout.

Spiders

Spiders live in my bones,
And they repopulate
Just as your cancer cells did,
But you didn't squirm around
When they joined up with other cells.
You sat and let them thrive,
Let them find home within your body.
You let them party inside the skin
You so desperately wished wasn't on anymore.
While I picked at the spider eggs
That sat on my arms,
You let your plague eat you up,
One organ failure at a time,
One last wish at a time,
Until the cancer won.

Sympathy

My graduating year
I received flowers as sympathy cards.

When my name wasn't called to wear the crown,
I stood on stage with a yellow rose,
That was supposed to promote optimism
And friendship,
But I felt isolated,
And so unimportant
That I let the flower wither in a vase,
Where every rose has gone to die in my care.

After my final concert
I unpinned the carnation from my chest
And watched how it wilted throughout the songs
That summed up my final moments
On the stage where I had been born.

The bouquet handed to me at my final recital
Had flowers that melted from the stage lights
And a thick layer of tap dust
That reminded me of newspaper print
Where my name was the next day
For years of dedication
And pointe shoe blisters.

After six months of love
A dozen roses found home in my locker
Until I was sure they'd make it home safe
Without a judgmental gaze,
But before they found relief in my vase,
They suffered through textbook abuse
And the smell of worn socks.

I'm waiting for the day I receive flowers
Out of curiosity
And purity,
And not as a worn down sentiment
That dies just as fast
As the flowers do.

Gold

A defaced heart
That beats for any connection,
Waits for glitter
To turn to gold,
And for meaningless words
To turn into love songs
Will hope that the gold can stay,
Even after it's corroded.

Afloat

I've drowned enough time in your eyes
To know I cannot swim,
But I am persistent
Because how else will I learn
How to stay afloat.

Freedom

Each night,
Claws drag me from my bed
Pull me onto the floor,
And fill me with dread
That leaks out of my eyes,
Staining my clothes an opaque black.
The monsters sit next to me,
Watch me weep,
Both arms around my back,
With claws forcing me down into the carpet,
As a reminder that I am not free,
And I never was.

Marigold

His hands are marigold roots
That plant happiness
In any spot he ventures to,
And his heart is a blooming sun
Which we all want to possess,
But whether to take the flower with us,
Or leave it in its place
Is what we consider.

Room 141U

I found the safety and warmth of a home
My freshman year of high school
Within sound proof walls
And the faint smell of valve oil
That lingered
Despite the constant changing of air fresheners.

I used to hide in the rows of chairs
Just to escape from the world
And feel a little closer to the music
That I so desperately wanted to master.

The room was an open canvas
That I got to paint every other morning
With harmonious tones
And light articulations,
But after doing that same thing for so long,
I lost the passion I used to find within,
And I lost that invincible feeling
I used to be drenched in.

The stress of improvement
Was a weight that was pulled my shoulders
Down to the ground
And slowed each movement
When I tried to get away
From the toxicity
Of repetition.

I never fell back in love with that room,
Even when the pressure dissolved,
But I still call it my home
Because if there's anywhere I belong
It's in the band room
Where my dreams did come true,
Once upon a time.

Lavender/Lilac

I can tell by the way you look at me
That my words don't mean the same to you
As they do to me,
And the colors I see
Aren't the same as yours.

He Loves Me Not

I fell in love with a boy
Who could never love me back,
Because who can love someone
Who cries when canaries fly
And daisies bloom.

Abandoned

I strolled along the curved roads for many winter
evenings.
I would always find myself lost within the
ambiance,
Without any place else to escape to.
Each time I passed through, the landscape would
change.
There were new trees and dampened snow drifts.
I remembered to appreciate them for all their
beauty.
I tried to appreciate them for some of their beauty.

I lost the race with the hills.
They kept rolling, but I couldn't keep up,
So I distanced myself from the hidden corners,
And ventured into the open space
Where leaves could not protect me from
The brutal chill of February.

Once spring arrived,
I took my time to feel reborn.
I took my time to learn everything I could about us.
Once the snow abandoned the scene.
I learned I did not want to be there.
I did not want to feel isolated.
I did not want to feel shackled to one spot.
So just as the snow did,
I abandoned the scene.
I left it alone to the spring showers.
I left it alone to the May flowers.
I left you alone.

Shower

I used to stand in the shower for hours
Hoping the water would burn all my skin off
Because then I'd be gone
And I wouldn't have to feel that hot water
anymore.

Yellow Canaries

Every morning my mother would hum
The birds are singing
The sun is shining
And it's time to say good morning,
And she'd assume I was happy
And alive
Like those small canaries that sat on our back
porch,
But I am not a bird,
Free to roam the sky
And view everything without biased eyes.

Water Lilies

I read between your words
Like I read between the brushstrokes
Of my favorite paintings.
I find what I want in the water lilies
And leave out the parts,
Like the floating algae,
I simply can't accept.

Habits

I lay back and feel the water fill my lungs.
The bliss of not being able to breathe
Washes over my body
Soaks into my limbs
And settles into my lungs.
Adrenaline
Replaces the blood
And I am left with a buzz
That reminds me of springtime bees
In my garden,
And I get up,
Empty the bathtub
And turn to drying myself off.
Just like I do every other night.

Prince Eric

I once met a boy,
Who reminded me constantly,
That he was a prince.

His blue eyes were ocean waves
That warned me to leave before
The tsunami came,
But his touch allowed me to settle into sand
And build castles for him
That were far more extravagant
Than anyone could dream up.
He was a divine ruler
Of my mind,
And knew just what to say
So I'd do what he asked me without
A third thought.
He invited me to parties
Where music would play
And he'd lay the bass drum beats
In front of me so I could consume
The propaganda at my own pace,
But I wasn't in control,
And I wasn't allowed to feel anything
Unless he wanted me to.

He crowned me his princess,
But only for a time
Before another hopeless girl
Floated his way.
She was just as naive as I was
And I wanted to warn her
But under his reign
I could no longer speak my mind,
Only tell her how wonderful he had been,
How we didn't work out
Because I wasn't fit to be queen.
And I had to watch them fall in love
And take the crown I thought I deserved
Off my head and be placed on hers.
He had left me to learn
The art of moving on
And growing up
Without the independence
He had stolen from me,
And he left couple girls
To do the same.

Instead of Blood

Blue soap runs through my arteries
In attempt to clean me
Of the sins I have committed,
But I cannot be cleaned
Of the words scratched into my skin
By those who have molasses
Instead of blood.

Red Hair

I remember the day
You told me you liked me perfectly.
Your jacket was around my shoulder,
And the warmth of winter fled my system.
Your red hair reminded me
Of all the blood that raced through my
Adrenaline flooded heart,
And all I wanted was for time to stop,
Because I knew it wouldn't last.
And it didn't
When you told me you didn't like me
That way.
But I can recall how nice it felt,
And how beautiful I felt,
And how safe the moment
Was tucked away inside of my brain.
I tried to move on,
And I'm still trying.

Lorain County

You moved to a new city
Three months after you met me.
You told me you miss this part of you,
But didn't clarify the city,
Or me.

Mindless

I wanted to tell you I love you,
But the words held my vocal chords hostage,
Tied them with broken capillaries,
And beat them until sores lined my throat
Where tonsils swelled
And nerves buzzed with adrenaline.
And I cannot tell you how wonderful
You make me feel
Because I am a victim of the forced silence
I surround myself in every night
When you ignore my messages.

Tulips

I found a lover
In my grandma's garden
That sprouts weeds
Just as often as it sprouts
Tulips.

Under Water

There's water that inhabits my ears
And it won't leave no matter
How hard I shake my head,
And it makes me feel full
Of falsely positive courage
And sour candy
That burns your tongue.
It's warm and comforting,
And somewhat peculiar in a sense,
Because having your brain drowning
In something other than knowledge
Isn't something one
Should experience.

Destined

I handed my fate to the stars
And asked them to decide what to do with my life,
And they responded with a pair of brown eyes
as deep as puddles,
And spotted with dim stars
That no longer lived in the sky.

bloom.

Yellow

Strawberry red sunglasses with yellow lenses
Filter out the grey and highlight
Forgotten childhood memories
That wait in black plastic bags
Thrown away before garage sales,
And after moving signs.
Yellow lenses illuminate the sun
That burns ghostly skin
On humid summer days
That allow for water balloon fights
To continue until the dusk has swept past
And brought up foul memories of
Fights with darts as punctuation.
I hid behind yellow lenses
In fear that those darts
Would hit me once again
And I truly believe that nothing can touch me
Behind me yellow lenses,
But just because you can't see the grey
Doesn't mean it's not there.

Robert

A golden man invited me into his rose family,
And to a tuft of flowers in October
Where we became acquainted with the night once
again.
We lived within the sound of trees,
And danced with the fireflies in the garden,
And when all went wrong in those winter months
We still had our Christmas trees
Covered in a dust of snow.
That night, instead of avoiding the road not taken,
We stopped in the woods on a snowy evening
Finding the time to talk,
And mended the walls that closed our hearts off.
I'd like to think we complemented each other
Like fire and ice,
But I am only a child of your metaphors.

Millennium

Sound waves stick themselves
To the freshly painted walls
Where tiny handprints lie,
And the paint ends up on my thighs,
Like bruising handprints
That remind me of the emotional fatigue of
Childhood,
And a summer suburbia
When country music was all the rage
And parenting wasn't as easy
As handing charged explorers
To kids who can't read.

Grey Suit

At the age of 62,
My father bought his first suit.
He walked into the house
With a weak smile
That told me something was wrong.
He asked me if I liked it,
And it didn't mean much to me then,
He was trying to say,

Do you think this suit would look nice on me
When I'm at my best friends' funeral,
And I have to hold myself together
Within this grey stitching?

Do you think this suit would look nice on me
When I'm in my casket,
And I'm no longer here to protect you
From grey thunderstorms?

Do you think this suit would look nice on me
When I am dead,
And this is all I have?

Renaissance

The couples dance around me in Italy,
And I am alone to my stained glass heart
And empty love boat,
That floats down dried up rivers
Where red lovers cannot part
But instead, avoid the tragic sensation
Of swallowing your pride alone
On a cold day in September
In a beautiful city.

If you can find symphonies

If you can find symphonies within the raindrops
    And sing along to the thunder melodies,
If you can speak in rhymes
    That don't have a language barrier
    And cannot be mistranslated,
If you can sing in empty hallways
    Where everyone knows your name,
If you can tell suede from leather
    Just by the way it sounds,
If you can feel your heartbeat
    In your ears and in your fingertips
    Even on sunny days,
If you can pull words out of the air
    And form majestic sentences
    That entrance even the wicked,
If you can push aside differences
    Eat the tension
    And shake hands,
If you can find heaven
    In the midday clouds
    And hell in the evening sun,

If you can see rainbows,
        In empty alleys and abandoned street cars,
If you can feel bombs in your chest
        When she says she doesn't love you
        anymore
        And still be able to look someone in the eyes
        the next day,
        You are a blue jay,
        In a world full of pigeons.

Happiness

Sometimes I try to imagine
What happiness must feel like.
Yellow fluffy blankets,
And soft kisses from small puppies,
And warm lavender tea,
And moonlit sand between your toes,
I imagine it feels like being filled
With packing peanuts
And unwavering hope.

Static

We talk in static now.
The indecipherable buzzes connect us.
It used to feel like butterflies swarming,
But now it feels like small shocks,
And somehow without any fight
I let the memories stay,
I let the pain stay,
Because I don't know any different.

Femininity

I struggle to find home
In dresses with open sides
And straps too small to fit on hangers
That hug all the wrong places
And wrinkles before 11 am.
I feel disconnected from the femininity
I forced myself to accept
In elementary school
When I'd wear a skirt to class,
But run to the bathroom at the first bell
To change into shorts
I had in my bag for soccer practice.
I'd paint my nails pink
In hope it'd cast a spell
To make being a girl more comfortable
But everyone should know
The tomboy you grew up with
Doesn't grow out of that phase,
But instead becomes numb
To originality, and susceptible
To the toxic femininity
Of roses and glitter.

Centered

Every time 2:13 am rolls around,
I can feel myself fall a little closer
To the center of the earth,
Where the dinosaur bones float in lava,
And where I can finally find warmth
In the early morning.

Vincent

I pictured you under that starry night
Without a thought or a will to live,
But instead an imagination that cannot be
Tied down
Like tree roots in an open wheat field.
You painted self portraits
That resembled sunflowers and olive trees
But I saw past your tired eyes and vibrant yellows.
I wish we could've met at the cafe one night,
Or maybe the yellow house you spent some time
in,
To talk over how it all happened,
But I guess when I'm gone, too,
We'll meet at eternity's gate,
And we can bathe in the comfort of irises and
almond blossoms.
For now I'll dream of your bedroom in Arles
Surrounded by an orchard blooming,
And take you for who you think you are,
And who you've become to me.

Continuum

If walls could speak,
My house would tell stories
Like we used to
Under the midnight sky
That connect the stars
To our ancestors,
With a single continuous line.

14-556

I woke up one morning in June
And let the sun wash me
Of all the thrills from past lives
I wish I'd gotten to experience
First hand,
Like throwing the first brick
On that sacred street.

My parents had asked
Why I looked so new,
So joyful,
But there was no way to explain it
To minds surrounded by concrete borders
So thick that they can't accept how revolutionary
June 26, 2015 was to someone like me
Who has been fighting for equality
Since I could breathe.

Falling in Love

The sky is endless,
And the stars are iridescent.
The wheels turn while gravel flies behind us.
I feel the frigid air flow through the windows,
And cover my skin in damp moonlight,
Relieving the stress of my bones
After a never ending day.

The stars settle into their own cars,
Following closely,
Altering their paths as we go
While the moon watches over,
Like an overbearing mother,
Protecting us from each danger that lay ahead.

She encourages us to keep our pace
To allow ourselves to get to know each
And every road that lies ahead
Everything,
And nothing is invisible in front of us.

I whisper into the unknown,
I want to die here
And I do,
Or at least a part of me does,
And each night
That piece goes farther into the sky
Joining the stars on our journey.

Sunrise

The pastels that once inhabited my mind
Grew into neons
That begged me to take over the world,
Starting with you.

Wasps

A nest of wasps
Have lived outside my house
Much longer than
I have lived inside.
They protect their young
Just as my mother protected
Me from them
When I was three
And interested in their yellow stripes
That reminded me of my favorite
Bumblebee stuffed animal.
They still live with me
And I have grown to appreciate
How they protect me
From the childlike curiosity
That still inhabits me
When I poke at their home
And hope they don't come
Chasing after me.

Reclaim

My body is not mine.

It belongs to a society
That preys on virginity,
And sexualizes children
That still shop at Justice.

It belongs to a society
That believes cat calls
Are compliments,
But compliments should be criminalized.

It belongs to the boy
Who watches me get out my car every day,
And sometimes takes pictures
When my shorts don't meet dress code.

It belongs to the girl
Who is supermodel thin
And watches me walk by
With an unconscious effort to prove she better than
me.

It belongs to a society
That decided my gender before I could speak,
And force fed me pink chiffon
Topped with feminine silence.

I belong to the men
Who believe they own me,
And the women
Who are glad they aren't me

Apocalypse

When the robots take over,
Let them know how much we loved this world.
How we'd create collections of art to show the
public for free,
How we'd sing our words when the world got
too exciting,
How we'd laugh at lonely daisies and pick them
so we remembered that moment,
How we'd walk the streets in the sun for a
moment to ourselves,
How we'd smile at strangers on the street,
How we'd encourage the ones we know to   follow
their dreams,
How we'd visit gardens with the ones we loved,
How we'd share our lives with one another online,
How we'd sing along in grocery stores when our
favorite song came on,
How we'd dance with our friends in the early
morning to songs we knew as kids,
How we'd do anything in our power to make our
lives,
And other lives better.

When the robots take over,
Let them know how much we cared.

Weeds

I am not a flower.
My skin isn't a blush rose
That lies like a shimmer over my freckles.
My feet are not roots
That ground me
And provide me with all I'll ever need.
My hair is not yellow pollen,
Free to roam and adventure,
To find a new start.
I am not a flower.

I am a weed.
My thoughts fill fields with poison
And I cannot be killed,
By words,
Or by my own self destruction
Because I am a weed,
And weeds prosper.

Bloom

I want to bloom like spring roses
At dance recitals
Where the air smells of hairspray
And lungs are filled with glitter dust
That joins the dirt of empty dressing rooms,
Where young girls find passion in pirouettes
And loneliness in backstage warmups
That fail to prepare you for an audience,
Where proud parents have camcorders
And little siblings squirm in chairs
That have seen more war than love,
Where sequins and hair pieces have flown away
And lonely jazz shoes hide in corners
That no one looks for.

NICOLE CLOYD has always had a passion for the art of poetry. When not writing furiously on any paper, or napkin they can get their hands onto, they like to play music, create art, and spend time with their friends. Nicole lives in Omaha, Nebraska and is attending college in Lincoln, Nebraska to get a degree in Art History. *Bloom* is Nicole's debut book.

Made in the USA
Lexington, KY
16 June 2018